Animal TECH

FUR & CLAWS

Tessa Miller

full tilt PRESS

Fur & Claws
Animal Tech

Copyright © 2019

Published by Full Tilt Press
Written by Tessa Miller
All rights reserved.

Printed in the United States of America.

Full Tilt Press
42982 Osgood Road
Fremont, CA 94539
readfulltilt.com
Full Tilt Press publications may be purchased for educational, business, or sales promotional use.

Editorial Credits
Design and layout by Sara Radka
Edited by Renae Gilles
Copyedited by Kristin J. Russo

Image Credits
Getty Images: background, cover, Blend Images, 27, DigitalVision, 25, 29, 30, EyeEm, 3 (cat), 13, 18, 26, 29 (detail), 35 (detail), EyeEm Premium, 15, georgeclerk, 31, iStockphoto, 1, 3 (syringes), 3 (sheep), 4, 6, 7, 8, 10, 11, 11 (detail), 14, 16, 17, 19, 20, 21, 22 (detail), 22, 23, 23 (detail), 24, 28 (detail), 28, 32, 34, 34 (detail), 40 (detail), 43, 45, kokouu, 5, Moment RF, 3 (polar bear), 12, 35, 44; NASA, 37, 39, 41; Newscom: imagebroker/ Rolf Nussbaumer, 36, Jonathan Alcorn/ZUMAPRESS, 33, NHPA/Photoshot, 10 (detail), Ringo Chiu/ZUMAPRESS, 38, Science Photo Library, 9, WENN.com, 42; Shutterstock: cover, 40, 41 (detail); Wikimedia, 16 (detail)

ISBN: 978-1-62920-739-1 (library binding)
ISBN: 978-1-62920-779-7 (eBook)

CONTENTS

Scientists searching for ways to improve hypodermic needles are looking at porcupine quills for inspiration.

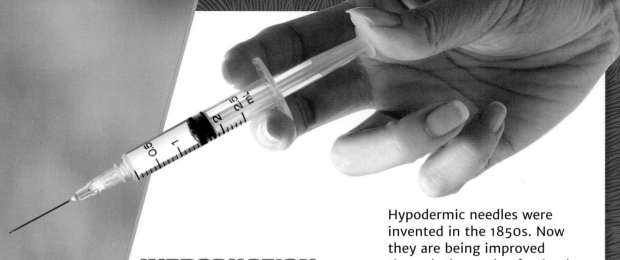

Hypodermic needles were invented in the 1850s. Now they are being improved through the study of animals.

INTRODUCTION

There are more than 5,000 **species** of mammals on Earth. Mammals are animals with fur. They have live babies they nourish with milk. They can fly, swim, run, crawl, jump, and hover. Some can even lay eggs. This **diversity** is why scientists often look to mammals for ideas. They use these ideas to help solve problems and create new technology. This is called biomimicry. "Bio" means "life." Mimicry is when you copy something else. Mammals have inspired advances in all fields of **technology**. By studying animals, Doctors have improved **vaccines**. Mammal fur has helped make man-made fabrics warmer. Robotic arms have been improved by studying elephant trunks. Scientists also study people to improve technology. By studying the human brain, they improved CAT scan machines. These machines can now map emotions. Right now, scientists are looking at many mammals for ideas. They want to help people live longer, healthier, better lives.

---

species: a group of plants or animals with similar features

diversity: variety; the state of being made up of many different things

technology: tools and knowledge used to meet a need or solve a problem

vaccine: a medicine that protects people against a disease

FUR WITH BURS

VELCRO

Cockleburs may be annoying, but they won't harm animals unless they are swallowed.

The company VELCRO now makes 35,000 different products.

Have you ever gone out walking with your dog and noticed small pieces of plants sticking to his legs? This happened to Swiss **engineer** George de Mestral.

One day, de Mestral returned from a hike. He noticed **cockleburs** stuck to his dog's fur. He became curious about them. The burs were able to hold fast. But they could be pulled off fairly easily. He decided to study them.

Burs can latch and unlatch from fur very easily. But it took him years to understand how they worked. Once he did, he decided to make a version himself. After 14 years of work, he invented Velcro in 1955. "Velcro" comes from two French words, *velour* and *crochet*, which mean "velvet" and "hook."

---

engineer: a person who plans and builds tools, machines, or structures

cocklebur: a flowering plant with round, spiky pods that hold its seeds

LESSONS FROM NATURE

The outside of a cocklebur is covered in thousands of little hooks. Tangled animal fur forms tiny, soft loops. When an animal brushes against a cocklebur, the hooks fasten onto the soft loops. Velcro is made of two sides. One side has hook-like barbs. The other one has soft loops. The two sides latch when they are pressed together.

The tiny hooks on a cocklebur allow it to latch onto an animal. When the animal scratches or bites it off, or brushes against something else, the bur falls to the ground.

The tiny nylon hooks on Velcro give a secure grip that also lets go easily.

At first, de Mestral made Velcro to replace zippers and buttons on clothes. Both sides were made of cotton. But the cotton hooks gave out after a few uses. De Mestral and his team thought that nylon would be stronger. They were right. Today's nylon hooks last longer and hold better. But Velcro can still be improved. In 2010, the United States military decided to switch back to buttons on uniforms. Velcro is too noisy when it is ripped apart. The makers of Velcro are working on ways to make it quieter.

DID YOU KNOW?
Astronauts use Velcro in space to hold equipment in place while in zero gravity.

TECH IN ACTION

Velcro mimics the unique way that cockleburs attach to animal fur.

HOOKS
Each cocklebur has small hooks that attach to an animal's fur.

TANGLES
Animals' fur tangles together to create small loops.

ATTACH & RELEASE
The animal might accidentally carry the cocklebur to a new place. If it drops off the animal, the bur can grow into a plant.

BARBS
Barbs on one side of the Velcro act like hooks.

LOOPS
The other side of Velcro is made of thousands of tiny loops.

LATCHING
When Velcro is pressed together, the hooks and loops latch. When Velcro is pulled apart, the link is broken.

POLAR BEARS

FABRIC

Polar bears are only found in the Arctic, in the Northern Hemisphere.

Many fabrics are made of man-made materials, such as nylon, velvet, and polyester. Others are made of natural materials, including cotton, silk, and wool.

Imagine if the world were completely covered in ice and snow. Temperatures everywhere would be **sub-zero**. What if humans only had their skin and hair to keep warm? Everyone would freeze! Humans do not have very thick hair on their bodies. Their skin doesn't offer much protection, either. That's why people wear clothes. They need to wear a lot of layers to stay warm in.

But polar bears use a different approach. They have a special type of fur to keep them warm. The bear can live in temperatures that drop below -40° Fahrenheit (-40° Celsius). Clothing designers have studied polar bear fur to create a new fabric. The fabric has the ability to keep people warm without being bulky.

---

sub-zero: temperatures below freezing, or 32°F (0°C)

Thanks to their fur and a 4-inch (10-centimeter) layer of fat underneath their skin, polar bears are able to keep nearly all of their body heat from escaping.

LESSONS FROM NATURE

The polar bear's fur is made of two layers. The inner layer is soft and downy. It prevents the bear's body heat from escaping. The outer layer is made of long "guard hairs." These are hollow and trap air inside. This increases the polar bear's **insulation**. In this way, polar bears can stay warm when the temperature is very cold.

The United Kingdom company HotSquash was able to mimic polar bear fur. They used it to design their ThinHeat fabric. The fabric is made of two layers. The bottom layer is made of solid thread. It traps a person's body heat. The top layer is made of hollow threads. This layer provides extra insulation. These two layers are woven together. Small holes in the fabric also let heat escape from a person's body when the air temperature is hot. This keeps the person cool. ThinHeat fabric helps a person **regulate** their temperature like a polar bear, without a lot of bulky clothing.

insulation: the ability to trap heat, electricity, or sound

regulate: to control

Wearing multiple thin layers of clothing keeps people warmer than wearing one or two thick layers. This is because more air is trapped between the many thin layers, improving insulation.

TECH IN ACTION

A UK company has created a fabric that works much like polar bear fur.

OUTER LAYER
The outer layer of polar bear fur is made of hollow guard hairs. They hold air and provide insulation.

INNER LAYER
The inner layer of fur is soft, trapping the polar bear's body heat.

THIN
The inner and outer layers are relatively thin, allowing the polar bear to move easily and quickly.

OUTER LAYER

An outer layer of hollow-core fibers traps air for greater insulation.

INNER LAYER

An inner layer of fibers is thinner but solid. This helps the material feel softer. It also helps trap the body heat of the person wearing the material.

LIGHTWEIGHT

When combined, the two layers of fabric are still thin. This creates a fabric that is lightweight and not bulky.

CAT'S EYES

ROAD REFLECTORS

Cats cannot see in complete darkness. But they can see well in one-sixth of the amount of light that humans need to see.

Road reflectors do not glow in the dark. They need light to make them shine.

Ever since cars were invented, people have been trying to make roads as safe as possible. The lines on the road divide it into lanes. Different colored lines tell people which side to drive on. This keeps cars from running into each other. But at night or in bad weather, it can be difficult to see these lines.

In 1930, Percy Shaw was driving at night in Halifax, England. The fog was very thick. He was having trouble seeing the curves of the road. Then his headlights flashed into a ditch. They caught the eyes of a cat. Shaw noticed something odd. The cat's eyes reflected the light of his headlights.

Shaw realized that **reflectors** along the roadside could help drivers stay safe. He invented "cat's eye" reflectors. Now, reflectors line most highways and roads in the United Kingdom and United States.

reflector: a piece of plastic or glass that is meant to shine light back at the viewer

LESSONS FROM NATURE

Cats' eyes have an extra lens that bounces light back out of the eyes. This lens helps the eyes collect more light in the dark. The lens is called the *tapetum lucidum*. Not all animals have this lens. Humans, pigs, kangaroos, and squirrels don't have it. But cats, dogs, deer, cows, horses, and ferrets all do.

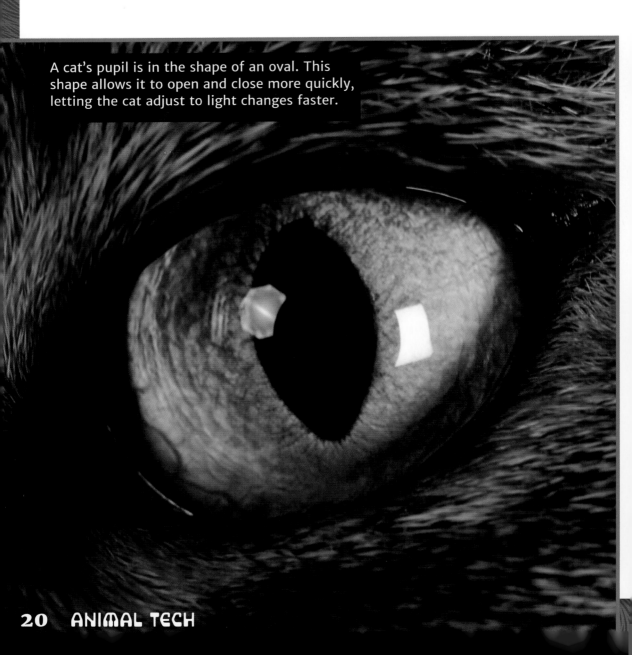

A cat's pupil is in the shape of an oval. This shape allows it to open and close more quickly, letting the cat adjust to light changes faster.

A road reflector does not have a smooth surface. Instead, its surface is shaped into many small facets, or angles. This creates more surface area for light to bounce off.

The first reflectors were flat. They were made from glass. But they often broke and needed to be replaced. After studying the *tapetum lucidum*, scientists were able to improve road reflectors. Their special **honeycomb** design reflects even more light back than flat reflectors. Now the reflectors are made from heavy plastics. The plastic is cheaper to make. So when reflectors break, road crews can easily replace them. Today, there are new designs being made. Engineers hope they will someday work better in foggy and blizzard conditions.

DID YOU KNOW?
Scientists are also looking at cats' tongues for ideas on how to make hairbrushes that detangle hair better than current brushes.

honeycomb: a pattern of six-sided shapes called hexagons

TECH IN ACTION

A nighttime encounter with a cat led to the invention of "cat's eyes" road reflectors.

LARGE
Cats' eyes are very large compared to the size of their heads.

LENS
Cats have a special lens called the *tapetum lucidum*. It reflects light.

GLOWING
People are able to see the light reflected off the tapetum lucidum. It is what makes cats' eyes seem to glow.

NOTICEABLE
Road reflectors are large enough to be seen from a moving vehicle.

FACETS
Reflectors have many facets that allow more light to bounce off.

REFLECTING
When a car's headlights shine onto the reflectors, they bounce light back. This guides people when driving.

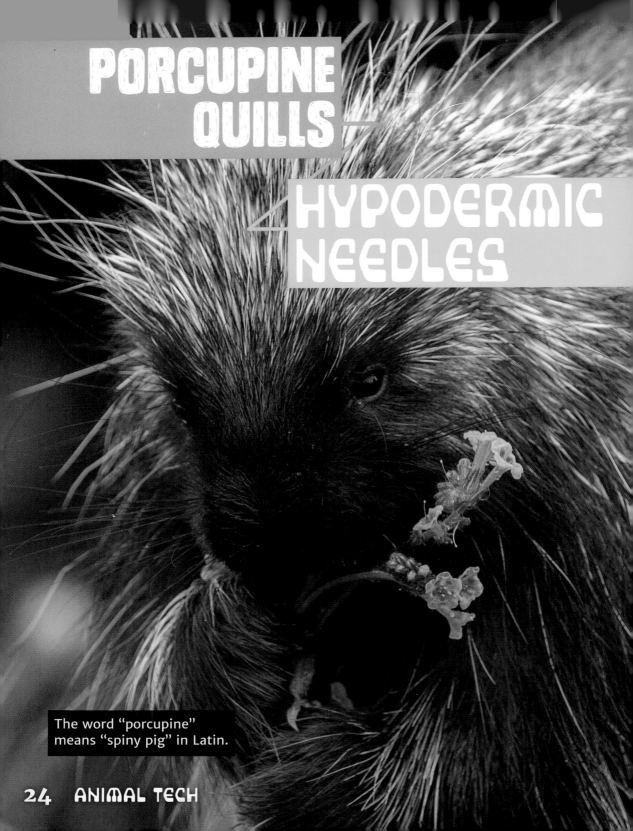

PORCUPINE QUILLS —

HYPODERMIC NEEDLES

The word "porcupine" means "spiny pig" in Latin.

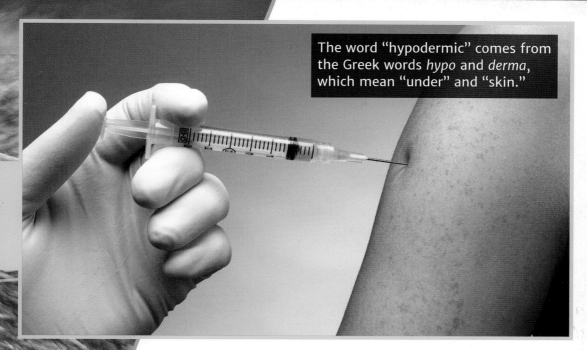

The word "hypodermic" comes from the Greek words *hypo* and *derma*, which mean "under" and "skin."

A friend is sick. They have a high temperature. They are either really cold or really hot. They can't eat anything because they just throw it up. They should go see the doctor. But they won't. Why? Because they are afraid the doctor will give them a shot. The thought of the needle piercing their skin scares them. They know a shot might make them feel better. But they just can't face the needle!

People who are afraid of needles often suffer from a **phobia** called **trypanophobia**. Doctors think that 1 in every 10 people suffers from this phobia. The pain of a shot is often what people fear the most. But scientists are trying to come up with a solution. They are working on a needle that is pain free. Which animal did they look at for inspiration? The North American porcupine.

phobia: an intense fear of something specific

trypanophobia: an intense fear of needles

LESSONS FROM NATURE

Each North American porcupine has more than 30,000 quills. The tip of each quill is covered in tiny barbs. There are more than 800 barbs per quill. When a porcupine is threatened, it only needs to lightly tap or brush against the other animal. The quills cut through the skin of a **predator** easily. And they stick there.

Getting stuck with porcupine quills can lead to infections deep under the skin.

Hypodermic needles are used to draw blood and to inject medicine and vaccines.

Doctors at Harvard University in Cambridge, Massachusetts, are studying these quills closely. They want to mimic them. They hope to design a smaller and sharper needle. They are even testing one of their designs now. The new needle has tiny barbs on the tip. The tiny barbs let the needle slide into the skin so easily, it does not cause pain. The biggest problem is that the barbs keep the needle stuck. To solve this problem, doctors are designing another needle. It would be made out of a material that dissolves. This needle would be pain free.

DID YOU KNOW?
In the United States, children receive an average of 50 vaccines by the age of 18.

predator: an animal that hunts or eats other animals

TECH IN ACTION

A porcupine uses its quills to protect itself from predators. Doctors are mimicking the quills to make better hypodermic needles.

BARBS
The tips of a North American porcupine's quills are covered in tiny barbs.

PAINLESS
The barbs pierce skin without causing much pain.

REMOVAL
The barbs hold the quill in place, making removal very painful.

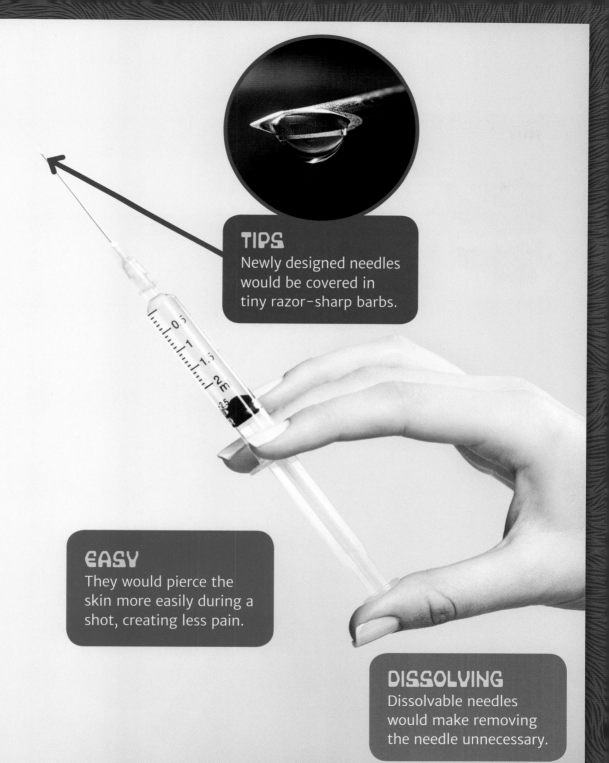

TIPS
Newly designed needles would be covered in tiny razor-sharp barbs.

EASY
They would pierce the skin more easily during a shot, creating less pain.

DISSOLVING
Dissolvable needles would make removing the needle unnecessary.

BONES

BUILDINGS

A dog has an average of 319 bones in its body.

A modern house might have 500–1,000 boards used to build its frame.

Broken bones are no laughing matter. Luckily for mammals, their bones heal quickly. Mammal bones are very unique. They are strong, but flexible. This is a special combination. It means these bones can go through a lot of **stress** before they break.

Mammal bones aren't completely solid. Under a microscope, they look more like a sponge. There are millions of tiny holes in them. These holes are filled with materials that act like a cushion. This helps keep bones from breaking. Bones also resist breaking because of how they are arranged in the body.

Engineers are hoping to make building materials that are strong like bones. Engineers have been studying all sorts of mammals to find the perfect design. Some day, they hope buildings can be built from bone-like boards. Engineers would arrange the boards in a similar way to how bones are found in the body.

stress: force or pressure

LESSONS FROM NATURE

Mammal bones are made of **calcium** and **collagen**. The combination of these two materials gives mammals' bones an advantage. If bones were made only of calcium, they would be very heavy. They would also break very easily. If they were made of collagen, they would bend too easily. However, calcium and collagen work perfectly together.

If engineers can successfully create bone-like building material, anything built out of that material would be able to bend under stress. Buildings with structures that mimic mammal skeletons would be very strong. This would be extremely helpful in earthquake zones. The buildings would bend and move with the earthquake. They wouldn't break and crumble.

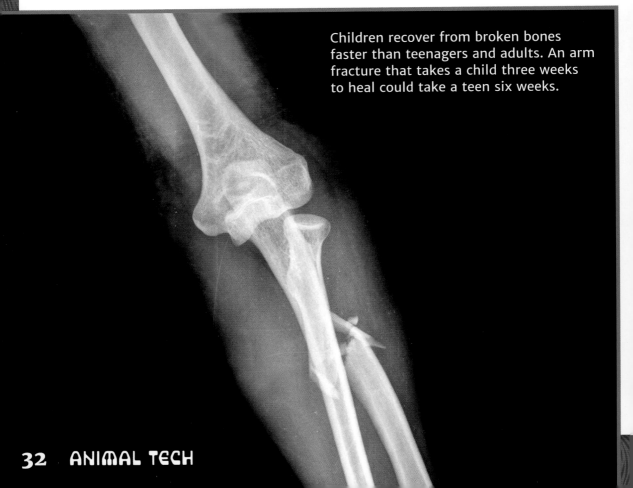

Children recover from broken bones faster than teenagers and adults. An arm fracture that takes a child three weeks to heal could take a teen six weeks.

The 1994 Northridge earthquake in California is considered the most expensive in US history. It caused an estimated $44 billion in damages to buildings and roads.

Just like real bones, new building materials would be able to "heal" themselves. If a crack forms, it would start a chemical **process**. A liquid would be released. It would act like a glue and seal the crack.

DID YOU KNOW?
At birth, the human body has about 270 bones. Many fuse together, so adults only have 206 bones.

calcium: a basic element found in many kinds of rocks, as well as the bones and teeth of animals

collagen: a basic substance found in the skin, muscles, organs, and bones of animals

process: a series of changes that happen one after another

TECH IN ACTION

Engineers are imagining a world where buildings are made of materials that mimic mammal bones.

HOLES
Mammal bones have millions of tiny holes in them.

FLEXIBILITY
Bones made out of calcium and collagen bend under stress.

DIFFERENT SIZES
A mammal's body has bones that are all different shapes and sizes.

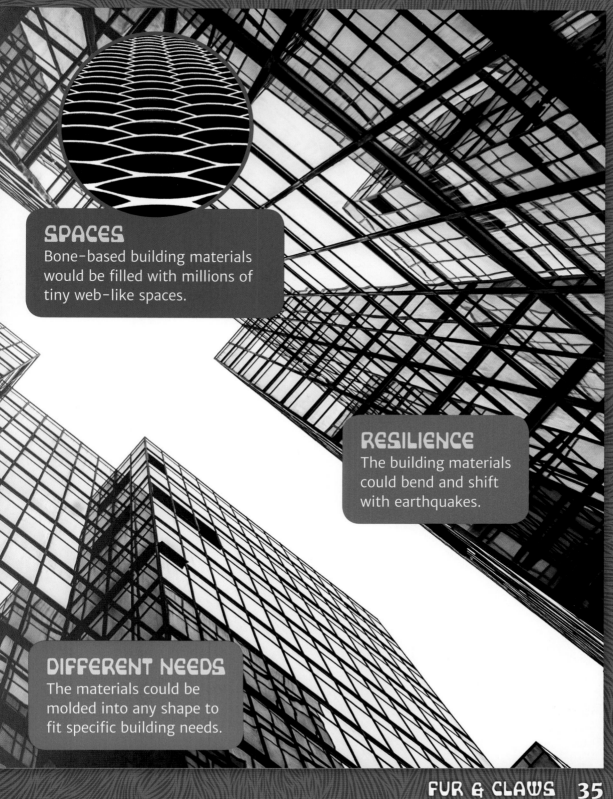

SPACES
Bone-based building materials would be filled with millions of tiny web-like spaces.

RESILIENCE
The building materials could bend and shift with earthquakes.

DIFFERENT NEEDS
The materials could be molded into any shape to fit specific building needs.

GOPHERS

DRILLING MACHINES ON MARS

Pocket gopher tunnels are usually 2.5 to 3.5 inches (6.4 to 8.9 cm) wide.

A hole dug on Mars in 2013 was 2.5 inches deep (6.4 cm).

Farmers deal with a lot of **pests**. Insects can destroy a whole field of crops in minutes. Small mammals are also dangerous for crops. One such mammal is the pocket gopher. These animals dig underneath the ground. They eat plants from the roots up. By the time a farmer realizes there's a problem, the plants are dead.

Pocket gophers are unique among mammals. They can dig perfectly round holes. They also dig complicated tunnel systems. They build entire networks underground. Pocket gophers can also dig through tough soil and rock. Gophers are often considered pests. But these powerful diggers have proven to be helpful when it comes to biomimicry.

Scientists have landed **rovers** on Mars. Now they are studying what the planet is made of. To do that, they need to drill through rock. This is not an easy thing to do. So engineers have teamed up with biologists to study pocket gophers.

---

pest: an insect or animal that damages crops, food, etc.

rover: a small vehicle used to explore extreme places such as the surface of a planet or moon

LESSONS FROM NATURE

The gopher's front teeth are very large. Gophers use them to loosen dirt and rocks as they dig. Unlike human teeth, these teeth never stop growing. A pocket gopher's claws are also very strong and sharp. They use powerful muscles in their forearms to dig. Their back legs kick the dirt out of the way. These traits make pocket gophers **efficient** digging machines.

Scientists are designing a drill that mimics pocket gophers. The drill **bit** is driven by a small but powerful motor. The drill bit's shape mimics a gopher's teeth and claws. Other drills need a separate machine to remove dirt. But this gopher-inspired drill collects the dirt as it spins. It then moves the dirt out of the way. Scientists call this machine the Auto-Gopher. In the future, they hope to send it to Mars, Jupiter's moon Europa, and Saturn's moon Enceladus.

Pocket gophers dig systems of tunnels that cover up to 2,000 square feet (186 square meters). That's about the size of a tennis court!

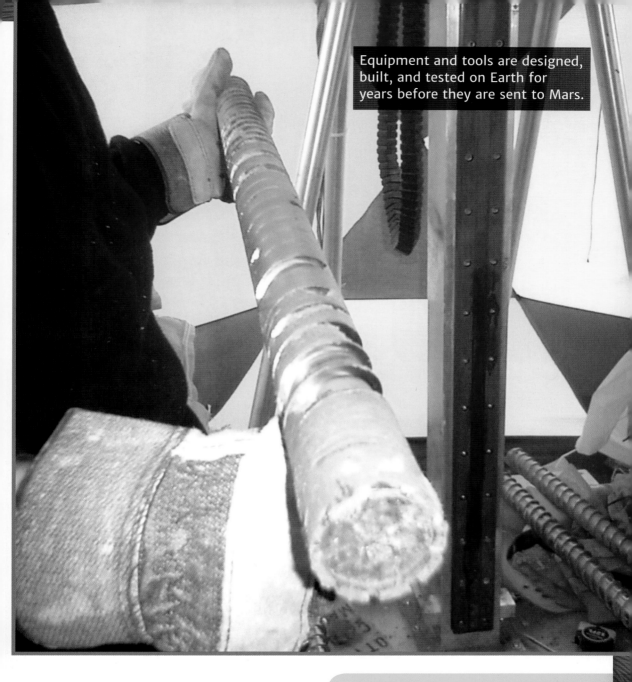

Equipment and tools are designed, built, and tested on Earth for years before they are sent to Mars.

efficient: able to succeed without wasting time or material

bit: the tip of a tool that is used to cut or drill

TECH IN ACTION

On Earth, gophers dig extensive tunnels underground. A new drilling machine would drill holes in a similar way, but on Mars.

COORDINATION
The gopher's strong forearms and back legs work together to dig and move debris out of the way at the same time.

STRENGTH
A pocket gopher's front teeth never stop growing. This means that they never wear out.

COMPLEXITY
Gophers can dig miles of tunnels underground in complex burrows.

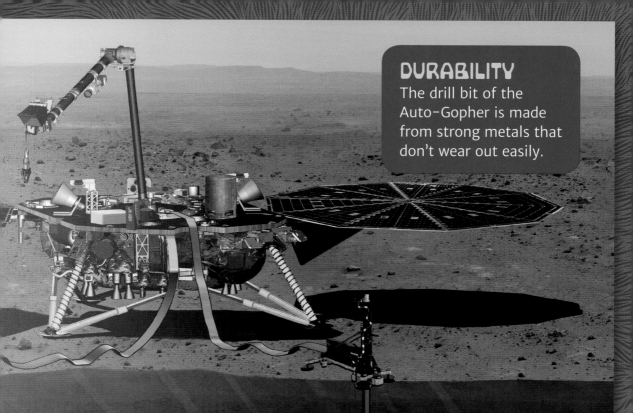

DURABILITY
The drill bit of the Auto-Gopher is made from strong metals that don't wear out easily.

EFFICIENCY
As the drill bit moves forward, it cuts and collects soil to get it out of the way.

DEPTH
The Auto-Gopher can reach farther underground than the drills used on Earth to dig wells.

FUR & CLAWS

CONCLUSION

Many scientists and engineers are
excited about the future of mimicking
mammals to create new robots.

Future scientists might use biomimicry to solve problems on other planets.

Biomimicry is a growing **industry**. By 2025, it could be worth more than $300 billion. Thousands of jobs could be created in the coming years. Many of these jobs in the biomimicry field may be different than they are now. Some will be completely new.

These days, skyscrapers and houses are built with wood and steel. Someday, construction workers could be building them out of bone-like materials. New, thinner fabric could keep people warm in the coldest places on Earth. Future explorers wouldn't have to wear bulky coats. Doctors could treat patients with shots and injections with a needle that doesn't hurt. Reflectors could line the tunnels being dug under the surface of Mars by thousands of Auto-Gophers.

The sky really is the limit. The future holds many opportunities for biomimicry. The next time there is a problem to be solved, take a look at nature for the solution.

industry: a group of businesses involved in making similar things

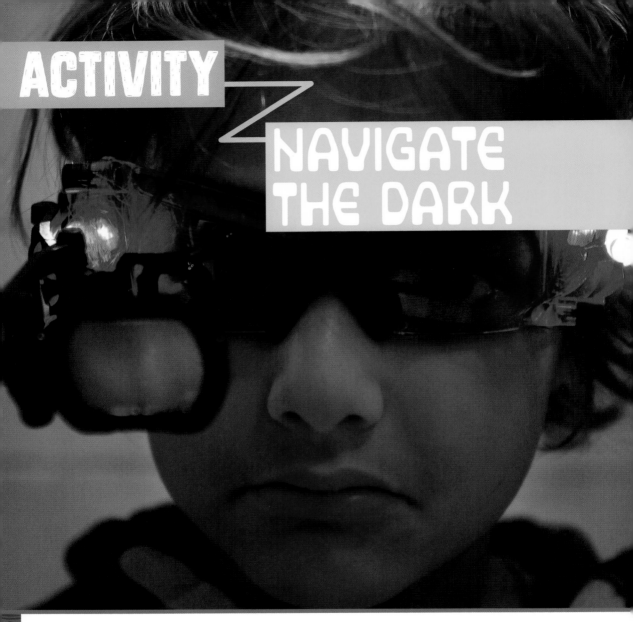

ACTIVITY

NAVIGATE THE DARK

Cats and other animals are able to switch between light and dark places quickly. That is because of the *tapetum lucidum* lens. Even though humans don't have that special lens, their pupils will eventually widen to allow more light in. This makes it easier to navigate in the dark. People just can't do it as quickly as a cat. Here's an experiment to help you explore navigating in the dark.

WHAT YOU NEED

- Friends or classmates, and a helpful adult
- An eyepatch for each person
- A room where you can turn off the lights for complete darkness
- Soft obstacles that won't hurt to bump into, such as bean bags or soft chairs
- A stopwatch
- Paper and pencils

WHAT TO DO

1. As a group, design an obstacle course or maze out of the large, soft obstacles. Make sure to put in lots of surprise twists and turns.

2. Run each person through the obstacle course and time how fast they can complete it. Write down the results.

3. Turn off the lights and time each person going through the obstacle course again. Make sure that you turn on the lights after each person has gone through the course in the dark.

4. Compare times. Were people able to complete the course in the dark? Discuss what made it more challenging.

5. Have everyone put on an eyepatch. Leave it on one eye for 15 minutes.

6. Turn off the lights again and have one person switch the eyepatch to the opposite eye. Run that person through the course. This time, do not turn the lights on in between participants.

7. Take note of times and challenges again. Turn on the lights and discuss your results. Was it easier with or without the eyepatch? Why? Did allowing one eye to adjust to the dark help improve each participant's time?

GLOSSARY

bit: the tip of a tool that is used to cut or drill

calcium: a basic element found in many kinds of rocks, as well as the bones and teeth of animals

cocklebur: a flowering plant with round, spiky pods that hold its seeds

collagen: a basic substance found in the skin, muscles, organs, and bones of animals

diversity: variety; the state of being made up of many different things

efficient: able to succeed without wasting time or material

engineer: a person who plans and builds tools, machines, or structures

honeycomb: a pattern of six-sided shapes called hexagons

industry: a group of businesses involved in making similar things

insulation: the ability to trap heat, electricity, or sound

pest: an insect or animal that damages crops, food, etc.

phobia: an intense fear of something specific

predator: an animal that hunts or eats other animals

process: a series of changes that happen one after another

reflector: a piece of plastic or glass that is meant to shine light back at the viewer

regulate: to control

rover: a small vehicle used to explore extreme places such as the surface of a planet or moon

species: a group of plants or animals with similar features

stress: force or pressure

sub-zero: temperatures below freezing, or 32°F (0°C)

technology: tools and knowledge used to meet a need or solve a problem

trypanophobia: an intense fear of needles

vaccine: a medicine that protects people against a disease

READ MORE

Jenkins, Steve. *Animal Book: A Collection of the Fastest, Fiercest, Toughest, Cleverest, Shyest—And Most Surprising—Animals on Earth.* Boston: Houghton Mifflin Harcourt, 2013.

Holzweiss, Kristina. *Amazing Makerspace DIY Movers.* New York: Children's Press, 2018.

Leslie, Clare Walker. *Nature Connection: An Outdoor Workbook for Kids, Families, and Classrooms.* North Adams, Mass.: Storey Publishing, 2010.

Levine, Sara. *Bone by Bone: Comparing Animal Skeletons.* Minneapolis: Millbrook Press, 2014.

Mara, Wil. *From Cats' Eyes to . . . Reflectors.* Innovations from Nature. Ann Arbor, Mich.: Cherry Lake Publishing, 2013.

WEBSITES

http://www.wgcucuriouskids.org/biomimicry/
  Watch a video on biomimicry.

http://pbskids.org/loopscoops/velcro.html
  Learn more about the invention of Velcro.

https://www.sciencenewsforstudents.org/article/cool-jobs-pet-science
  Read about working in pet science.

https://kids.nwf.org/Home/Kids/Ranger-Rick/Animals/Mammals/Polar-Bears.aspx
  Explore the world of polar bears.

https://www.uspto.gov/kids/activities.html
  Play games and do activities about inventions.

INDEX